Napoleon Dynamite

THE COMPLETE QUOTE BOOK

BASED ON THE HIT FILM FROM FOX SEARCHLIGHT PICTURES
WRITTEN BY JARED HESS AND JERUSHA HESS

SIMON SPOTLIGHT ENTERTAINMENT
New York   London   Toronto   Sydney

The following quotes were taken from the final shooting script for *Napoleon Dynamite*, written by Jared Hess and Jerusha Hess.

This book is a work of fiction. Any references to historical events, real people, or real locales are used fictitiously. Other names, characters, places, and incidents are the product of the author's imagination, and any resemblance to actual events or locales or persons, living or dead, is entirely coincidental.

Edited by Emily Westlake

SIMON SPOTLIGHT ENTERTAINMENT
An imprint of Simon & Schuster Children's Publishing Division
1230 Avenue of the Americas, New York, New York 10020
SIMON SPOTLIGHT ENTERTAINMENT and related logo are trademarks of
Simon & Schuster, Inc.
Manufactured in the United States of America
10 9 8
Library of Congress Control Number 2005927731
ISBN-13: 978-1-4169-1391-7
ISBN-10: 1-4169-1391-2

CONTENTS

SPORTS AND RECREATION:

Wolverine Hunting, Drawing Warriors, and Other Activities

DON: "Hey, Napoleon. What'd you do last summer again?"

NAPOLEON: "I told you, I spent it with my uncle in Alaska hunting wolverines!"

DON: "Did you shoot any?"

NAPOLEON: "Yes, like fifty of 'em. They kept trying to attack my cousins! What the heck would you do in a situation like that?"

DON: "What kind of gun did you use?"

NAPOLEON: "A freakin' twelve gauge, whaddya think?"

PEDRO: "It's a Sledgehammer."

NAPOLEON: "Dang! Lucky. You ever take it off any sweet jumps?"

NAPOLEON: "You got like three feet of air that time."

KIP:

"It'd be nice if you could pull me into town."

REX.

"Bow to your sensei. Bow to your sensei!"

"You think I got where I am today because I dressed like Peter Pan here?"

NAPOLEON: "What the flip was Grandma doing at the sand dunes?"

UNCLE RICO: "Hey, you guys wanna see my video?"

***

UNCLE RICO: "So, whaddya think?"

KIP: "It's pretty cool, I guess."

UNCLE RICO: "Oh man, I wish I could go back in time. I'd take state."

NAPOLEON: "This is pretty much the worst video ever made."

KIP: "Napoleon, like anyone can even know that."

UNCLE RICO: "You know what, Napoleon? You can leave."

NAPOLEON: "You guys are retarded!"

8

UNCLE RICO:

"How much you wanna make
a bet I can throw a football
over them mountains?"

NAPOLEON:

"You wanna play me?"

KIP:

"Napoleon, don't be jealous that I've been chatting online with babes all day. Besides, we both know I'm training to become a cage fighter."

NAPOLEON

"Well, I have all your equipment in my locker. You should probably come get it 'cause I can't fit my nunchucks in there anymore."

PEDRO: "Aren't you pretty good at drawing, like, animals and warriors and stuff?"

NAPOLEON: "Yes. Probably the best that I know of."

NAPOLEON:

"It took me, like, three hours to finish the shading on your upper lip.

It's probably the best drawing that I've ever done."

PEDRO:

"Did you draw her a picture?"

NAPOLEON:

"Heck yes I did!"

D-QWON:
"Welcome to D-Qwon's dance grooves. Are you ready to get your groove on?"

NAPOLEON:
"Yes."

NUTRITION:

Tots and Other Food Groups

GRANDMA:

"Make yourself a dang quesadilla!"

NAPOLEON:

"Fine!"

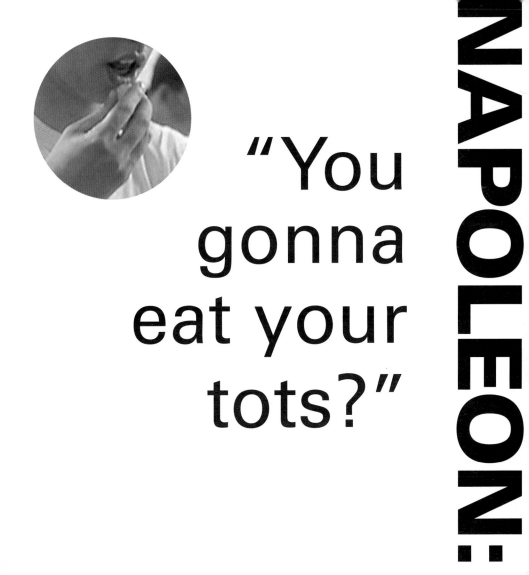

"You gonna eat your tots?"

NAPOLEON:

NAPOLEON:

"I see you're drinking one percent. Is that 'cause you think you're fat? 'Cause you're not. You could be drinking whole if you wanted to."

RANDY:

"Napoleon! Gimme some of your tots!"

NAPOLEON: "No! Go find your own!"

RANDY: "Come on, gimme some of your tots!"

NAPOLEON: "No! I'm frickin' starved! I didn't get to eat anything today!"

FASHION AND BEAUTY:

Boondoggle Key Chains and Other Must-Haves This Year

DEB:

"And here we have some boondoggle key chains, a must-have for this season's fashion."

PEDRO:

"I like her bangs."

NAPOLEON

"Me too."

PEDRO:
"Well, what are you going to wear to the dance?"

NAPOLEON:
"Just like a silk shirt or something."

NAPOLEON: "Pedro, how do you feel about that one?"

PEDRO: "It looks nice."

NAPOLEON: "Yeah, it looks pretty sweet. It looks awesome! It's incredible."

NAPOLEON:

"I like your sleeves. They're real big."

NAPOLEON: "Why do you got your hood on like that?"

PEDRO: "Well, when I came home from school my head started to get really hot. So I drank some cold water, but it didn't do nothing. So I laid in the bathtub for a while, but then I realized that it was my hair that was making my head so hot. So I went into my kitchen and I shaved it all off. I don't want anyone to see."

NAPOLEON: "I know what you mean."

NAPOLEON:

"That one's good. It looks like a medieval warrior."

DEB:

"I could wrap you in some foam, or something billowy?"

ANIMALS:

Ligers, Llamas, and Chickens—Oh My!

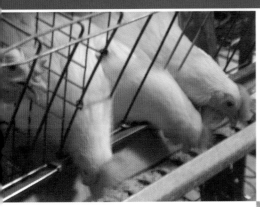

NAPOLION:

"Tina, you fat lard, come get some dinner!"

DEB: "What are you drawing?"

NAPOLEON: "A liger."

DEB: "What's a liger?"

NAPOLEON: "It's pretty much my favorite animal. It's like a lion and a tiger mixed, bred for its skills in magic."

NAPOLEON: "The defect in that one is bleach."

JUDGE: "That's correct."

NAPOLEON: "Yes!"

NAPOLEON: "This tastes like the cow got into an onion patch."

JUDGE: "Correct."

NAPOLEON: "Yes!"

"They're pretty good,
except for one little problem.
That little guy right there.
He is nipple number five.
A good dairy cow should
have, like, four."

35

NAPOLEON

"Tina! Come get some ham!"

NAPOLEON:
"Do the chickens have large talons?"

FARMER: "Do they have what?"

NAPOLEON: "Large talons?"

FARMER: "I don't understand a word you just said."

WORK AND MONEY:

Making Sweet Moola

UNCLE RICO:

"We also need some way to make us look official. Like we got all the answers."

KIP:

"How 'bout some gold bracelets?"

KIP.

"I'm making some sweet moola with Uncle Rico."

NAPOLEON:

"I can make that much money in five seconds!"

UNCLE RICO:

"Napoleon, looks like you don't have a job. So why don't you get out there and feed Tina?"

NAPOLEON:

"Why don't you go eat a decroded piece of crap?"

UNCLE RICO:

"Napoleon, you know we can't afford the fun pack. What, do you think money grows on trees in this family? Take it back! Get some Pampers for you and your brother while you're at it."

POLITICS:

Vote for Pedro

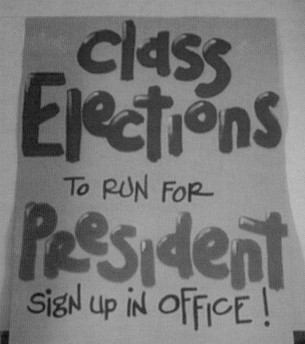

"Last week Japanese scientists explaced—placed—explosive detonators at the bottom of lake Loch Ness to blow Nessie out of the water. Sir Court Godfrey of the Nessie Alliance summoned the help of Scotland's local wizards to cast a protective spell over the lake and its local residents and all those who seek for the peaceful existence of our underwater ally."

NAPOLEON:

PEDRO: "Do you think people will vote for me?"

NAPOLEON: "Heck yes! I'd vote for you."

PEDRO: "Like, what are my skills?"

NAPOLEON: "Well, you have a sweet bike, and you're really good at hookin' up with chicks. Plus you're, like, the only guy at school who has a mustache."

PEDRO: "That's true."

NAPOLEON: "If you need to use any of my skills I can do whatever you want."

NAPOLEON:

"I'm voting for Pedro Sanchez. Who do you think?"

47

NAPOLEON

"Vote for Pedro."

NAPOLEON:

"Pedro offers you his protection."

PRINCIPAL:

"Look, Pedro. I don't know how they do things down in Juarez, but here in Idaho we have a little something called pride. Understand? Smashing the face of a piñata that resembles Summer Wheatley is a disgrace to you, me, and the entire Gem State."

PEDRO:

"I don't understand. He said you're not allowed to smash piñatas that look like real people. But we do it in Mexico all the time."

Presidente Pedro? Felicidades!

NAPOLEON:

"Just tell them that their wildest dreams will come true if they vote for you."

"Well, I never thought I would make it here today. I would make a great class president because I promise to put two new pop machines in the cafeteria, and I'm also gonna get a glitter Bonne Bell dispenser for all the girls' bathrooms. Oh, and we're gonna get new cheerleading uniforms. Anyway, I think I'd be a great class president. So, who wants to eat chimichangas next year? Not me. See, with me it will be summer all year long. Vote for Summer."

SUMMER:

PEDRO:

"Hello. I don't have much to say. But I think it would be good to have some Holy Santos brought to the high school to guard the hallway and to bring us good luck. El Santo Nino de Adoche is a good one. My aunt Goicha has seen him. And we have a great FFA schedule lined up. And I'd like to see more of that. If you vote for me, all of your wildest dreams will come true."

RELATIONSHIPS:

Cake Building and Other Ways to Get Babes

NAPOLEON:

"Do you dare me to go talk to her?"

NAPOLEON:

"Yeah, my old girlfriend from Oklahoma was gonna fly out here for the dance but she couldn't 'cause she's doing some modeling right now."

PEDRO

"Is she hot?"

NAPOLEON: "Have you heard about the dance?"

PEDRO: "Yes."

NAPOLEON: "Have you met anyone to ask yet?"

PEDRO: "No, but I probably will after school."

NAPOLEON: "Who are you gonna ask?"

PEDRO: "That girl over there."

NAPOLEON: "Summer Wheatley? How the heck are you gonna do that?"

PEDRO: "Build her a cake or something."

"Things are getting pretty serious right now. I mean, we chat online for, like, two hours every day. So I guess you could say things are getting pretty serious."

KIP:

"I'm just getting really, just kind of TO'd because she hasn't even sent me a full body shot yet."

NAPOLEON: "I don't even have any good skills."

PEDRO: "What do you mean?"

NAPOLEON: "You know, like nunchucks skills, bowhunting skills, computer hacking skills. . . . Girls only want boyfriends who have great skills!"

PEDRO: "Who was that?"

NAPOLEON: "Trisha."

PEDRO: "Who's she?"

NAPOLEON: "My woman I'm taking to the dance."

KIP·

"LaFawnduh is the best thing that has ever happened to me. I'm one hundred percent positive that she's my soul mate. Napoleon, I'm sure there's a babe out there for you too. Peace out."

NAPOLEON:

"I caught you a delicious bass."

SCHOOL:

Where I Spent the Worst Day of My Life

NAPOLEON:

"Hey, is that a new kid or something?"

"Yeah, there's, like, a buttload of gangs at this school. This one gang kept wanting me to join because I'm pretty good with a bowstaff."

NAPOLEON: "So me and you are pretty much friends by now, right?"

PEDRO: "Yes."

NAPOLEON: "So you got my back and everything?"

GRANDMA:

"How was school?"

NAPOLEON:
"The worst day
of my life,
whaddya think?"

EVERYTHING ELSE:

Gosh!

VERN:

"What are you gonna do today, Napoleon?"

NAPOLEON:

"Whatever I feel
like I wanna
do, gosh!"

NAPOLEON: "Can you bring me my Chap Stick?"

KIP: "No, Napoleon."

NAPOLEON: "But my lips hurt real bad!"

NAPOLEON:

"Ahhhhh. Kip hasn't done flipping anything today!"

NAPOLEON

"You don't have to stay here with us.
We're not babies."

CORRINA: "Bueno?"

NAPOLEON: "Hello?"

CORRINA: "Who's this?"

NAPOLEON: "Napoleon Dynamite."

CORRINA: "Who?"

NAPOLEON: "Napoleon Dynamite. I'm one of Pedro's best friends."

CORRINA: "Your name is Napoleon?"

DEB:

"Imagine you're weightless, in the middle of the ocean, surrounded by tiny little sea horses."

UNCLE RICO:

"Poor kid. I've been taking care of him while his grandma's in the hospital. He still wets the bed and everything. . . . He's a tender little guy."

NAPOLEON: "What the crap was Uncle Rico doing over at my girlfriend's house?"

KIP: "Napoleon, let go of me! I think you're bruising my neck meat."

NAPOLEON: "Fine. What the heck are you guys doing? Trying to ruin my life and make me look like a freakin' idiot?"

UNCLE RICO:

"I wish you wouldn't look at me like that, Napoleon."

NAPOLEON:

"I wish you'd get out of my life and shut up!"

TRISHA:
"Hi, is Napoleon there?"

NAPOLEON:
"Yes."

TRISHA:
"Can I talk to him?"

NAPOLEON:
"You already are."

NAPOLEON.

"So you guys are, like, Pedro's cousins
with all the sweet hookups?"

NAPOLEON:

"Are you guys having a killer time?"

KIP: "Yes!"

KIP: "It's a time machine, Napoleon. We bought it online."

NAPOLEON: "Yeah, right."

KIP: "It works, Napoleon. You don't even know."

***

NAPOLEON: "Ow! Ow! Ow! It kills! My pack! Ow! Turn it off! It's a piece of crap and it doesn't work!"

UNCLE RICO: "I coulda told you that."

DEB:

"I don't need herbal enhancers to feel good about myself. And if you're so concerned about that, why don't you try eating some yourself?"

NAPOLEON: "Everybody at school thinks I'm a freakin' idiot because of you!"

NAPOLEON:

"Grandma just called and said you're supposed to go home."

UNCLE RICO:

"She didn't tell me anything."

NAPOLEON: "Too bad. She says she doesn't want you here when she gets back because you've been ruining everybody's lives and eating all her steak."

NAPOLEON:

"Pedro, just listen to your heart. That's what I do."

INDEX